C000303501

Movie D

Sing Along with 8 Great-Sounding Tracks

Contents

Alfred Publishing Co., Inc.
16320 Roscoe Blvd., Suite 100
P.O. Box 10003
Van Nuys, CA 91410-0003
alfred.com

ISBN-10: 0-7390-4444-3 (Book and CD)
ISBN-13: 978-0-7390-4444-5 (Book and CD)

Cover Art:
Lights: © istockphoto.com/sweetandsour
Theatre: © Ted Engelbart
Microphone: © istockphoto.com/Abzee

Don't Rain on My Parade

From *Funny Girl*
Words by
BOB MERRILL
Music by
JULE STYNE

Don't tell me not to live, just sit and putter.
Life's candy and the sun's a ball of butter.
Don't bring around a cloud to rain on my parade.
Don't tell me not to fly, I've simply g ot to.
If someone takes a spill, it's me and not you.
Who told you you're allowed to rain on my parade?

I'll march my band out, I'll beat my drum.
And if I'm fanned out, your turn at bat, sir,
at least I didn't fake it, hat, sir,
I guess I didn't make it.

But whether I'm the rose of sheer perfection
or freckle on the nose of life's complexion,
the cinder or the shiny apple of its eye,
I gotta fly once, I gotta try once,
only can die once, right, sir?
Ooh, love is juicy, juicy and you see,
I gotta have my bite, sir.

Get ready for me, love, 'cause I'm a "comer."
I simply gotta march, my heart's a drummer.
Don't bring around the cloud to rain on my parade.

I'm gonna live and live now!
Get what I want, I know how!
One roll for the whole shebang!
One throw, that bell will go clang!
Eye on the target and wham!
One shot, one gun shot and bam!
Hey, Mister Arnstein, here I am!

I'll march my band out, I'll beat my drum.
And if I'm fanned out, your turn at bat, sir,
at least I didn't fake it, hat, sir,
I guess I didn't make it.

Get ready for me, love, 'cause I'm a "comer."
I simply gotta march, my heart's a drummer.
Nobody, no, nobody is gonna rain on my parade!

Don't Rain on My Parade

From *Funny Girl*

Words by
BOB MERRILL

Music by
JULE STYNE

Don't tell___ me not to live, just sit___ and put-ter. Life's can - dy and the

sun's a ball___ of but-ter. Don't bring___ a-round a_____ cloud to rain on my pa-

rade._____ Don't tell___ me not to fly, I've sim - ply got to.

If some - one takes a spill, it's me___ and not you. Who told___ you you're al -

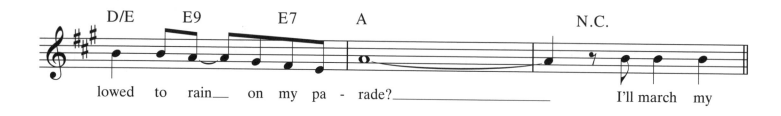

lowed to rain___ on my pa - rade?_____ I'll march my

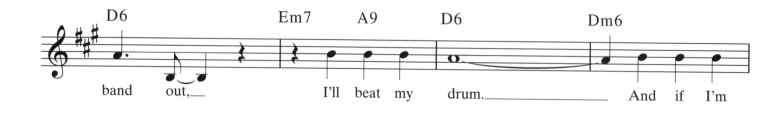

band out,___ I'll beat my drum._____ And if I'm

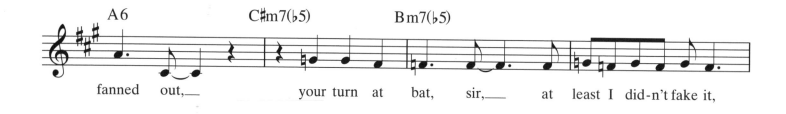

fanned out,___ your turn at bat, sir,___ at least I did-n't fake it,

hat, sir,___ I guess I did-n't make it. But wheth - er I'm the

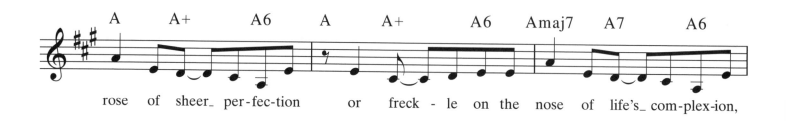

rose of sheer_ per-fec-tion or freck - le on the nose of life's_ com-plex-ion,

the cin - der or the___ shin - y ap-ple of its eye,_____

I got - ta fly once, I___ got - ta try once, on - ly can die once,

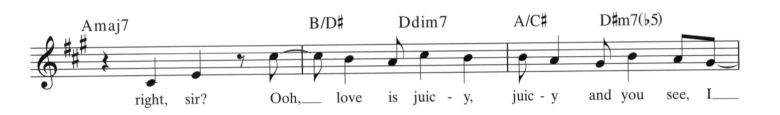

right, sir? Ooh,___ love is juic - y, juic - y and you see, I___

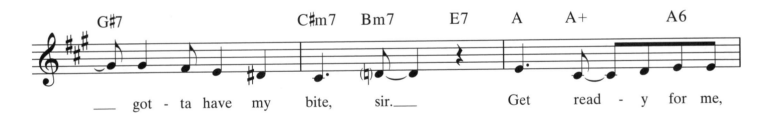

___ got - ta have my bite, sir.___ Get read - y for me,

love, 'cause I'm___ a "com-er." I sim - ply got - ta march, my heart's_ a drum-mer.

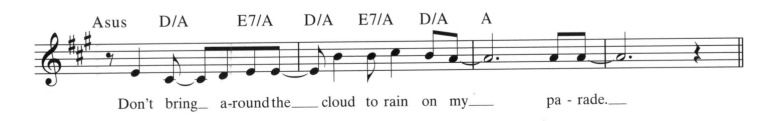

Don't bring_ a-round the___ cloud to rain on my___ pa - rade.___

I'm gon - na live and live now! Get what I

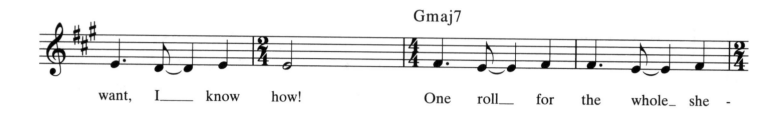

want, I know how! One roll for the whole she -

bang! One throw, that bell will go clang!

Eye on the tar - get and wham! One shot, one

gun shot and bam! Hey, Mis-ter Arn - stein, here I am!

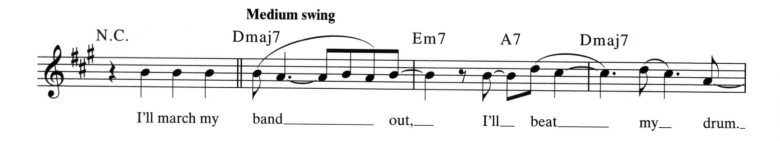

I'll march my band out, I'll beat my drum.

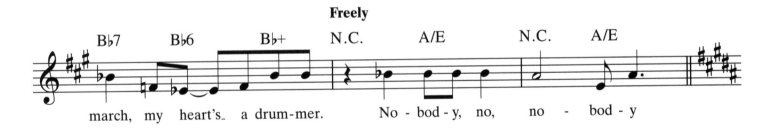

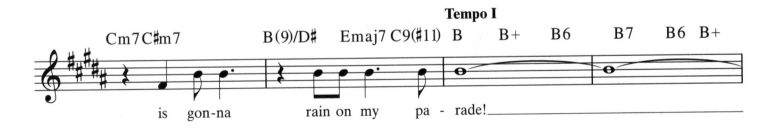

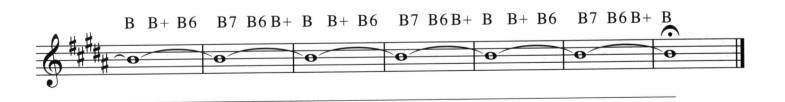

Evergreen

(Love Theme from *A Star Is Born*)

Words by
PAUL WILLIAMS
Music by
BARBRA STREISAND

Ah.
Love, soft as an easy chair;
love, fresh as the morning air.
One love that is shared by two
I have found with you.

Like a rose under the April snow,
I was always certain love would grow.
Love, ageless and evergreen,
seldom seen by two.

You and I will make each night a first,
ev'ry day a beginning.
Spirits rise and their dance is unrehearsed.
They warm and excite us
'cause we have the brightest love,
two lights that shine as one,
morning glory and the midnight sun.

Time we've learned to sail above;
time won't change the meaning of
one love, ageless and ever,
evergreen.
Ah.

Evergreen
(Love Theme from *A Star Is Born*)

Words by
PAUL WILLIAMS

Music by
BARBRA STREISAND

Ah.

Love,_____ soft as an eas - y chair;_____

love,_____ fresh as the morn - ing_ air._____

One_____ love that is shared by two_____

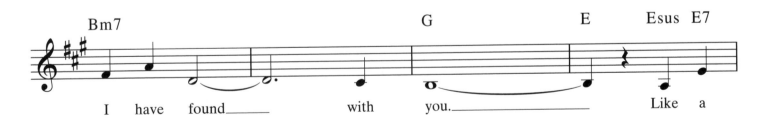

I have found_____ with you._____ Like a

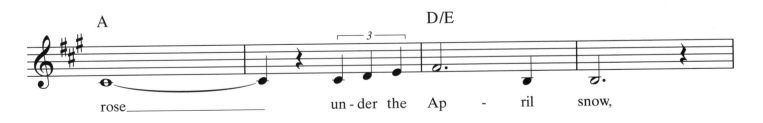

rose_____ un - der the Ap - ril snow,

Evergreen - 3 - 1
26496

love,_____ two lights that shine_____ as one,

morn - ing glo - ry and_ the mid - night_ sun._____

Time_____ we've learned to sail a - bove;_____

time_____ won't change the mean -ing of_____ one

love,_____ age-less and ev - er,_____

ev - er - green._____

rit.

_____ Ah.

Fame

From the M-G-M Motion Picture *Fame*
Lyrics by
DEAN PITCHFORD
Music by
MICHAEL GORE

Verse 1:
Baby, look at me
and tell me what you see.
You ain't seen the best of me yet.
Give me time; I'll make you forget the rest.
I got gold in me,
and you can set it free.
I can catch the moon in my hand.
Don't you know who I am?

Chorus:
Remember my name, (fame!)
I'm gonna live forever.
I'm gonna learn how to fly (high!)
I feel it coming together.
People will see me and die. (Fame!)
I'm gonna make it to Heaven.
Light up the sky like a flame; (fame!)
I'm gonna live forever.
Baby, remember my name.
(Remember, remember, remember, remember,
remember, remember, remember, remember.)

Verse 2:
Baby, hold me tight
'cause you can make it right.
You can shoot me straight to the top.
Give me love and take all I've got to give.
Baby, I'll be tough.
Too much is not enough.
I can ride your heart 'til it breaks.
Mmm, I got what it takes.

Chorus:
Remember my name, (fame!)
I'm gonna live forever.
I'm gonna learn how to fly (high!)
I feel it coming together.
People will see me and die. (Fame!)
I'm gonna make it to Heaven.
Light up the sky like a flame; (fame!)
I'm gonna live forever.
Baby, remember my name.
(Remember, remember, remember, remember,
remember, remember, remember.)

(Instrumental solo ad lib.)

Chorus:
Fame!
I'm gonna make it to Heaven.
Light up the sky like a flame; (fame!)
I'm gonna live forever.
Baby, remember my name.
(Remember, remember, remember, remember,
remember, remember, remember.)

Chorus:
Remember my name, (fame!)
I'm gonna live forever.
I'm gonna learn how to fly (high!)
I feel it coming together.
People will see me and die. (Fame!)
I'm gonna make it to Heaven.
Light up the sky like a flame; (fame!)
I'm gonna live forever.
People, remember my name.
(Remember, remember, remember, remember,
remember, remember, remember.)
Remember my name.

Fame

From the M-G-M Motion Picture *Fame*

Lyrics by
DEAN PITCHFORD

Music by
MICHAEL GORE

Moderately fast dance beat ♩ = 132

Verse:

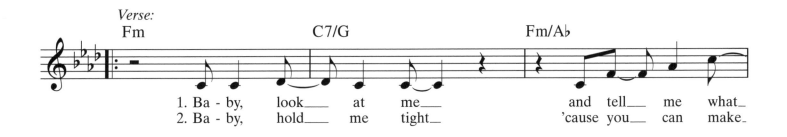

1. Ba - by, look___ at me___ and tell___ me what___
2. Ba - by, hold___ me tight___ 'cause you___ can make___

___ you___ see. You ain't seen___ the best___ of me yet.
___ it___ right. You can shoot___ me straight___ to the top.

Fame - 5 - 1
26496

_____ gon - na make_ it to Heav - en. Light up the sky_ like a flame;_

_____ (fame!) I'm gon - na live_ for - ev - - er.

Ba - by, re - mem - ber my_____ name. (Re - mem - ber, re - mem - ber,

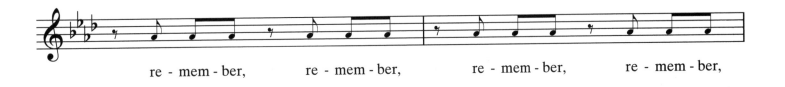

re - mem - ber, re - mem - ber, re - mem - ber, re - mem - ber,

re - mem - ber, re - mem - ber.)

re - mem - ber.)

Instrumental solo ad lib.:

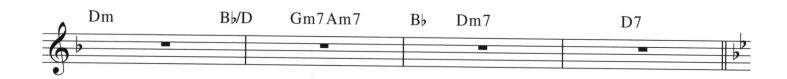

Chorus:

Fame! I'm___ gon - na make___ it to Heav - en.

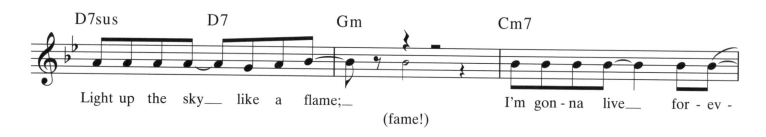

Light up the sky___ like a flame;___   I'm gon - na live___ for - ev -
(fame!)

er.   Ba - by, re - mem - ber my___ name.
(Re - mem - ber,   re - mem - ber,

re - mem - ber,   re - mem - ber,   re - mem - ber,   re - mem - ber,   re - mem - ber.)
Re - mem - ber my

name,   I'm gon - na live___ for - ev - er.
(fame!)

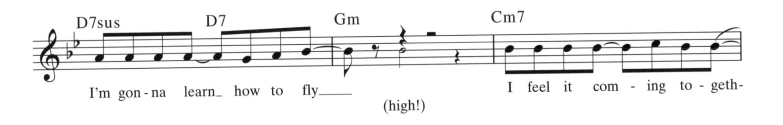

I'm gon-na learn_ how to fly_____ (high!) I feel it com - ing to - geth-

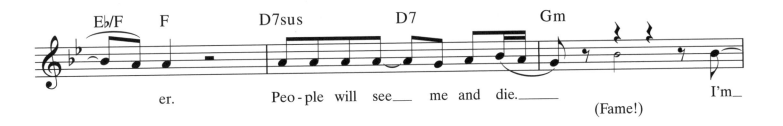

er. Peo-ple will see__ me and die._____ (Fame!) I'm_

__ gon-na make_ it to Heav - en. Light up the sky__ like a flame;_

__ (fame!) I'm gon - na live__ for - ev - er.

Peo-ple, re - mem - ber my__ name._____ (Re-mem-ber, re-mem-ber, re-mem-ber, re-mem-ber,

re - mem-ber, re - mem-ber, Re-mem - ber my name, re - mem-ber.)

I Believe in You and Me

From *The Preacher's Wife*
Words and Music by
SANDY LINZER and DAVID WOLFERT

Verse 1:
I believe in you and me,
I believe that we will be
in love eternally.v
Well, as far as I can see,
you will always be the one for me.
Oh, yes, you will.
And I believe in dreams again.
I believe that love will never end.
And like the river finds the sea,
I was lost, now I'm free,
'cause I believe in you and me.

Verse 2:
I will never leave your side,
I will never hurt your pride.
When all the chips are down, babe,
said I will always be around,
just to be right where you are, my love.
You know I love you, boy.
I will never leave you out,
I will always let you in, boy, my baby,
to places no one's ever been.
Deep inside, can't you see
that I believe in you and me?

Bridge:
Maybe I'm a fool to feel the way I do.
I will play the fool forever
just to be near you forever.

Verse 3:
I believe in miracles,
and love's a miracle.
And yes, baby,
you're my dream come true.
I, I was lost, now I'm free,
oh baby,
'cause I believe,
I do believe in you and me.
See I was lost, now I'm free,
'cause I believe in you and me,
believe in you and me.

I Believe in You and Me

From *The Preacher's Wife*

Words and Music by
SANDY LINZER and DAVID WOLFERT

Slowly ♩ = 63

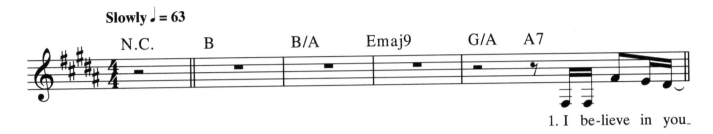

I Believe In You and Me - 4 - 1
26496

like the riv - er finds_____ the sea,_____ I___ was

lost,_____ now___ I'm___ free,_____ 'cause

I be - lieve_ in you___ and___ me. 2. I will nev - er leave

Verse 2:

your side,___ I will nev - er hurt___ your___ pride._ When all the

chips are down,___ babe,___ said I will al - ways be___ a - round,___

just to be right where you are,_____ my love.

You know I love___ you, boy. I will nev - er

leave you out,___ I will al-ways let___ you in,___ boy, my ba-by, to

plac-es no one's ev - er been.___ Deep___ in - side,___

___ can't___ you see___ that

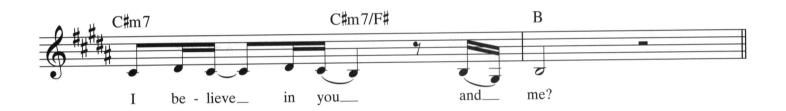

I be - lieve___ in you___ and___ me?

Bridge:

May - be I'm__ a fool___ to feel the way_ I do.___

I will play_ the fool_ for-ev - er___ just to be near you___ for-ev - er.___

Verse 3:

3. I be-lieve in mir - a - cles,___ and love's___

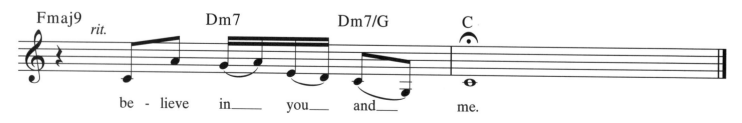

Theme from New York, New York

From *New York, New York*
Lyrics by
FRED EBB
Music by
JOHN KANDER

Start spreadin' the news,
I'm leaving today,
I wanna be a part of it,
New York, New York.
These vagabond shoes
are longing to stray,
and step around the heart of it,
New York, New York.
I wanna wake up
in the city that doesn't sleep
to find I'm king of the hill,
top of the heap.

My little town blues
are melting away,
I'll make a brand-new start of it
in old New York.
If I can make it there,
I'd make it anywhere,
it's up to you,
New York, New York.

New York, New York.
I wanna wake up
in a city that doesn't sleep
to find I'm king of the hill,
head of the list,
cream of the crop
at the top of the heap.

My little town blues
are melting away,
I'll make a brand-new start of it
in old New York.
If I can make it there,
I'd make it anywhere,
come on, come through
New York, New York.

Theme from
New York, New York

From *New York, New York*

Lyrics by
FRED EBB

Music by
JOHN KANDER

Medium swing ♩ = 112

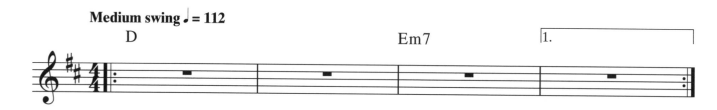

Start spread-in' the news,   I'm leav-ing to -

day,   I wan - na   be   a   part___ of it,

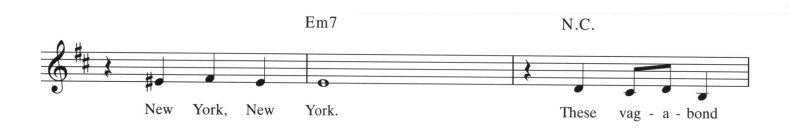

New York, New   York.   These   vag - a - bond

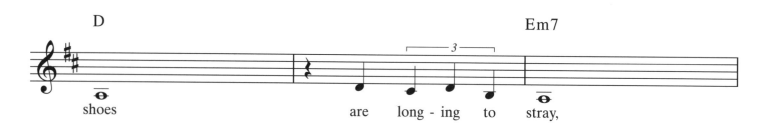

shoes   are   long - ing   to   stray,

Theme From New York, New York - 4 - 1
26496

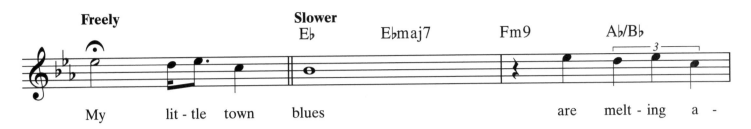

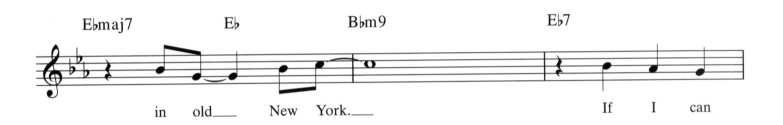

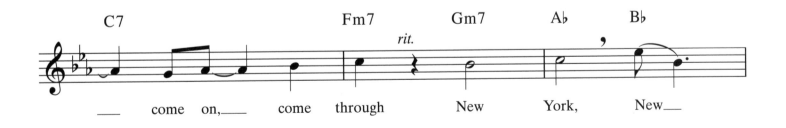

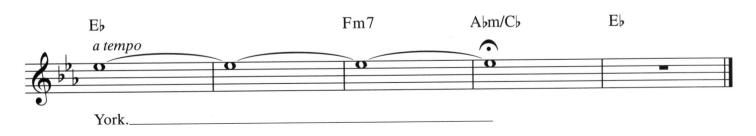

Theme From New York, New York - 4 - 4
26496

Over the Rainbow

From *The Wizard of Oz*
Lyric by
E.Y. HARBURG
Music by
HAROLD ARLEN

Verse 1:
Somewhere over the rainbow,
way up high,
there's a land that I heard of
once in a lullaby.

Verse 2:
Somewhere over the rainbow
skies are blue,
and the dreams that you dare to dream
really do come true.

Bridge:
Someday I'll wish upon a star
and wake up where the clouds are far behind me.
Where troubles melt like lemon drops
away, above the chimney tops,
that's where you'll find me.

Verse 3:
Somewhere over the rainbow
bluebirds fly,
birds fly over the rainbow,
why then, oh why can't I?

If happy little bluebirds fly
beyond the rainbow,
why, oh why can't I?

Over the Rainbow

From *The Wizard of Oz*

Lyric by
E.Y. HARBURG

Music by
HAROLD ARLEN

Moderately slow ♩ = 88

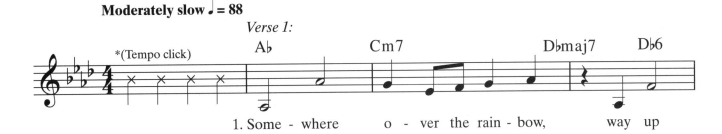

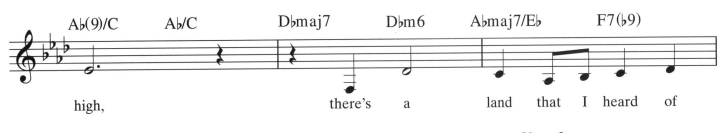

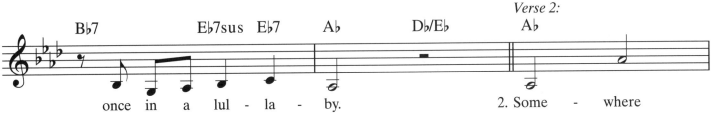

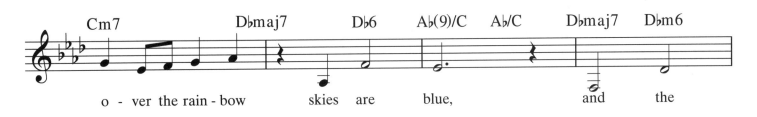

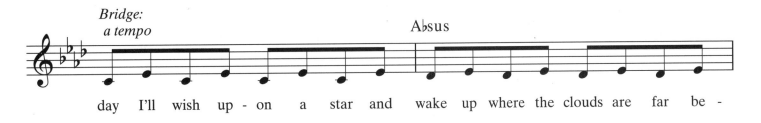

*A keyboard string chord is provided at the beginning of the play-along recording as a pitch reference for the vocalist.

Over the Rainbow - 2 - 1
26496

The Rose

From the Twentieth Century-Fox Motion Picture *The Rose*
Words and Music by
AMANDA McBROOM

Some say love, it is a river
that drowns the tender reed.
Some say love, it is a razor
that leaves your soul to bleed.
Some say love, it is a hunger,
an endless, aching need.
I say love, it is a flower
and you its only seed.

It's the heart afraid of breaking
that never learns to dance.
It's the dream afraid of waking
that never takes the chance.
It's the one who won't be taken,
who cannot seem to give,
and the soul afraid of dyin'
that never learns to live.

When the night has been too lonely
and the road has been too long,
and you think that love is only
for the lucky and the strong,
just remember in the winter,
far beneath the bitter snows,
lies the seed that with the sun's love
in the spring becomes the rose.

The Rose

From the Twentieth Century-Fox Motion Picture *The Rose*

Words and Music by
AMANDA McBROOM

Slowly ♩ = 63

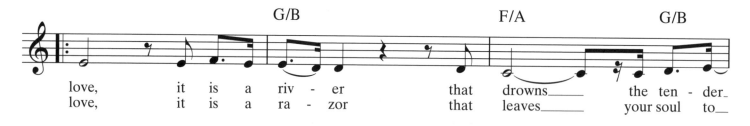

love, it is a riv - er that drowns____ the ten - der
love, it is a ra - zor that leaves____ your soul to

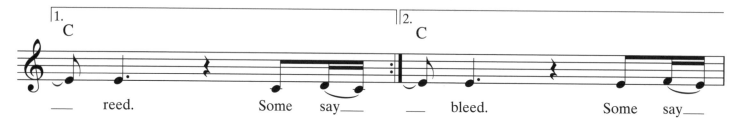

____ reed. Some say____ ____ bleed. Some say____

love,____ it is a hun - ger, an end - less, ach - ing

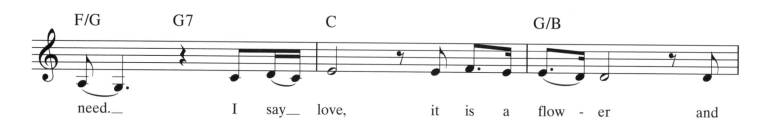

need.____ I say__ love, it is a flow - er and

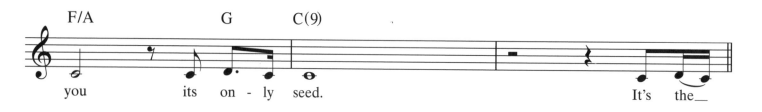

you its on - ly seed. It's the__

The Rose - 2 - 1
26496

The Wind Beneath My Wings

From *Beaches*
Words and Music by
LARRY HENLEY and JEFF SILBAR

Verse 1:
It must have been cold there in my shadow,
to never have sunlight on your face.
You were content to let me shine, that's your way,
you always walked a step behind.

Verse 2:
So I was the one with all the glory,
while you were the one with all the strength.
A beautiful face without a name for so long,
a beautiful smile to hide the pain.

Chorus:
Did you ever know that you're my hero,
and ev'rything I would like to be?
I can fly higher than an eagle,
for you are the wind beneath my wings.

Verse 3:
It might have appeared to go unnoticed,
but I've got it all here in my heart.
I want you to know I know the truth,
'course I know it,
I would be nothing without you.

Chorus:
Did you ever know that you're my hero,
you're ev'rything I wish I could be?
I can fly higher than an eagle,
for you are the wind beneath my wings.

Did I ever tell you you're my hero?
You're ev'rything, ev'rything I wish I could be.
Oh, and I, I could fly higher than an eagle,
for you are the wind beneath my wings,
'cause you are the wind beneath my wings.
Oh, the wind beneath my wings.
You, you, you, you are the wind beneath my wings.

Fly, fly, fly away, you let me fly so high.
Oh, you, you, you, you, the wind beneath my wings.
Oh, you, you, you, the wind beneath my wings.
Fly, fly, so high against the sky,
so high I almost touch the sky.
Thank you, thank you, thank God for you,
the wind beneath my wings.

The Wind Beneath My Wings

From *Beaches*

Words and Music by
LARRY HENLEY and JEFF SILBAR

Slowly ♩ = 63

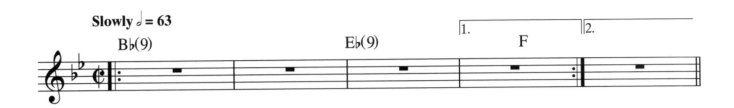

Verse 1:

1. It must have been cold there in my shad - ow,___

to nev - er have sun - light on your face.

You were con - tent to let me___ shine, that's your way,___

you al - ways walked a step___ be - hind.

36

2. So I____ was the one with all____ the glo - ry,
3. It might. have ap - peared to go____ un - no - ticed,

while you__ were the one with all____ the strength.
but I've__ got it all here in____ my heart.

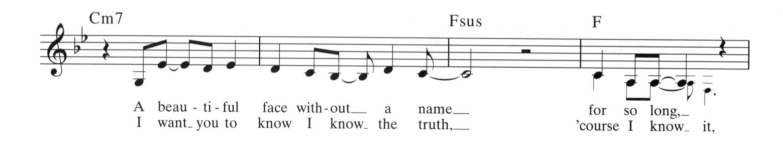

A beau - ti - ful face with-out__ a name____ for so long,__ 'course I know_ it,
I want_ you to know I know_ the truth,____

a beau - ti - ful smile to hide__ the pain.]
I____ would be noth - ing with - out you. ⌡

Chorus:

Did you ev - er know_ that you're my he - ro,

{ and ev - 'ry-thing I would like to____ be? }
{ you're ev - 'ry-thing I wish I could be.____ }

The Wind Beneath My Wings - 5 - 2
26496

I can fly high - er than an ea - gle,

for you are the wind be-neath my_____ wings.

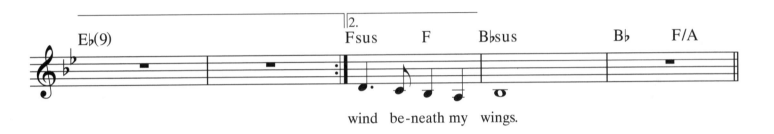

wind be-neath my wings.

Did I ev - er tell you you're my_____ he - ro? You're ev -

'ry-thing, ev - 'ry-thing I wish_ I could be._____ Oh, and I,_

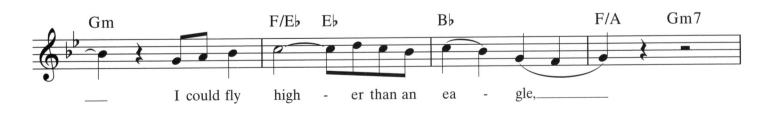

___ I could fly high - er than an ea - gle,_____

The Wind Beneath My Wings - 5 - 3
26496

for you are the wind be-neath my wings,

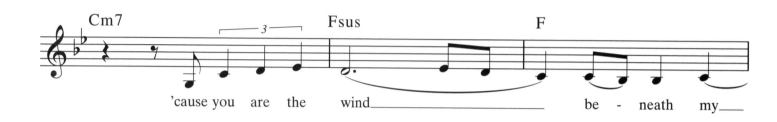

'cause you are the wind_____ be - neath my____

____ wings. Oh, the wind be - neath_ my__ wings._____

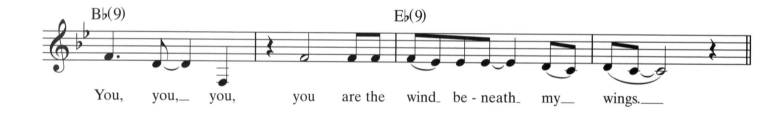

You, you,__ you, you are the wind_ be - neath_ my__ wings.___

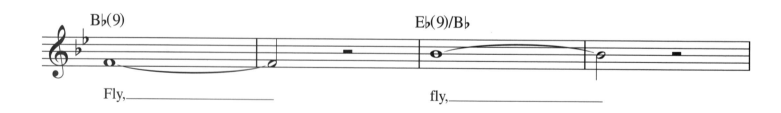

Fly,_____ fly,_____

fly a - way,____ you let____ me fly__ so__ high._ Oh,____